D0819062

Motivation & Goal-Setting
The Keys to Achieving Success

Written by Jim Cairo

A National Seminars Publications
Desktop Handbook

National Seminars Publications
A Division of Rockhurst College Continuing Education Center, Inc.

6901 West 63rd Street • P.O. Box 2949 • Shawnee Mission, KS 66201-1349
1-800-258-7246 • 1-913-432-7757

Motivation & Goal-Setting: The Keys to Achieving Success
Published by National Seminars Publications
© 1992 Rockhurst College Continuing Education Center, Inc.

Available to the trade exclusively from Career Press

Printed in the United States of America

1   2   3   4   5   6   7   8   9   10

ISBN 1-55852-065-1

Table of Contents

INTRODUCTION

This book is about how to achieve success. It is for both individuals and organizations because careful study shows that the process of achieving success is remarkably consistent from person to person and from organization to organization.

Success can be achieved by following an eight-step method that is clearly outlined in this book. These eight steps will provide you with a clear picture of your current situation and the means for achieving your personal goals on a day-to-day basis. Professionally, it is a valuable tool that will save you time and increase your efficiency and that of your organization.

Here is what the eight-step method will do for you:

- Help you understand yourself better.

- Assist you in identifying your personal and professional objectives.

- Help you clearly define your values and goals.

- Give you the means to achieve those objectives.

The eight-step method involves:

1. Examining your identity.

2. Defining your values.

3. Establishing goals.

4. Putting together an action plan.

5. Examining various facets of motivation.

6. Establishing discipline.

7. Maintaining flexibility.

8. Reaching an outcome.

Think of the eight steps as a road map. The outcome of your eight steps is your objective or the destination you targeted when you started on your journey toward success.

So, initially your road map looks like this:

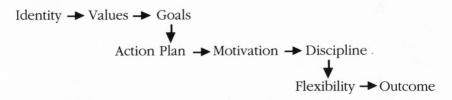

Identity → Values → Goals

Action Plan → Motivation → Discipline

Flexibility → Outcome

This handbook will show you how each of the eight steps fits into your road map for success and teach you how to use it to become more focused and productive. Along the way, we will look at these key issues in two areas: your personal life and your professional life.

ACHIEVEMENT: THE ROAD TO SUCCESS

In order to understand where you want to go on your journey to achieving success, let's look at the beginning and end of our road map.

Identity ⟶ Outcome

Identity

If you have no concept of your identity, then you have nothing on which to build your plans for the future. A lack of identity often results in a lack of direction. You must know your strengths and weaknesses; otherwise the process of defining your goals and working toward them will be flawed.

In Your Personal Life

The key question is: Who am I?

Your answer should be an accurate self-assessment that examines how others see you, how you choose to spend your time, the quality of your relationships, and your strengths, skills and weaknesses. It is an honest personal inventory.

In Your Professional Life

The key question is: Do my career and professional expectations mesh with the goals, expectations and identity of the company (or department) I work for?

This is an honest professional inventory. You can get so busy working, so tied up in urgent matters, policies and procedures, that you may no longer understand the role you (or your department) play in the organization and how those roles relate to the larger corporate identity.

Determining your professional identity is one of the most important and motivating business decisions you can make. When you develop an understanding of who you are professionally, you will become more productive, communicate better and greatly increase your opportunities for success.

Outcome

Outcome means achieving a desired result. The outcome is the destination of your journey. Don't be deceived into thinking that goals and outcome are the same – they are not. Goals are conceptual; the outcome is what actually happens, the tangible destination, which may or may not be the one you originally targeted on your road map.

In Your Personal Life

Achieving a desired outcome may mean learning new skills, improving your eating habits, completing the requirements for a college degree or improving your personal relationships.

In Your Professional Life

For your career, the end result may mean meeting production quotas, providing outstanding customer service, advancing your career or completing a project by a predetermined deadline.

You now have a clearer understanding of the beginning and end of your road map.

Identity ⟶ Outcome

There are a number of intermediate steps to be negotiated before you arrive at your outcome.

Values

After you identify who you are, it is necessary to reflect on your values. Values and identity are not the same. Values are what you hold dear, what you believe in, what you would like to represent. The more your identity reflects your values, the surer you can be of yourself. And the more you are true to your values, the more your personal and professional lives will be "in sync."

In Your Personal Life

Each person has a unique personality composed of individual experiences that creates something called "self." Your personal values are an extension of this self. These values govern your behavior toward other people, the types of relationships you seek, your attitude toward what is right and wrong, and your fundamental convictions. Successfully defining your personal values will make the journey to your outcome easier.

In Your Professional Life

The same is true in your professional life. Think about the "culture" that exists where you work.

- Are the ethics in harmony with yours?

- Are you proud of your company and co-workers?

- Does your job make you feel good?

You should enjoy (at least most of the time) your work. If you do not, then you must re-examine your values to determine why. Determining values involves soul-searching. There are many reasons why identity and values may be different. The greater the gap between them, the more likely you are to be unhappy or to under-perform in your career.

Your road map now has an additional step.

Identity ➔ Values ————————➤ Outcome

Once you have a clear concept of your identity and values, you have a foundation upon which to build your goals.

Goals

Achieving your goals doesn't guarantee personal or professional fulfillment. You can create an outcome that is empty if your goals aren't relevant to your personal life, your career or your job expectations. Worthy goals are based on values that are well thought out and honest.

To arrive at an outcome, you have to know your destination. It makes sense, doesn't it? But it's estimated that less than five percent of the population has clearly defined goals. Without them, you can't possibly progress down the road.

In Your Personal Life

Your mind contains a homing device similar to one in a guided missile. This homing device keeps you focused and moving toward your destination. Your goals direct your homing device. If you start to go off course, your goals will point you once again in the right direction.

Define your target. If you want to have a sense of purpose and accomplishment in your personal life, it is crucial that you have clearly defined goals.

In Your Professional Life

At work, you have to consider not only your career goals but also those of the company and of your supervisor. These added factors can make the determination of career goals very complex.

Enlightened companies know the importance of individual goals, and they share their plans and business objectives with employees in an open way. If you work in such a positive climate, you can set your goals so they are consistent with those of your organization. If your goals are not in alignment with your organization's goals, you should seriously consider a different job. Setting goals is your third step.

Identity → Values → Goals ⟶ Outcome

So far, the approach has been conceptual. Thinking is not doing, however. You must now identify those specific activities that will move you closer to your desired outcome.

Action Plan

Action plans are based on the information gleaned from defining your identity, values and goals, coupled with the effort you are willing to make to realize your intended result. You also need to look at your resources. You don't want to define an action plan that you are unable to implement because of inadequate time, energy or money.

In Your Personal Life

Examine your goals, list the steps you need to take and the resources required to accomplish these goals. Prioritize the steps. Now you know what is required to accomplish each of your goals. Are your goals realistic? Do you have the resources available to implement your action plan?

In Your Professional Life

If you want to accomplish a professional goal or get something done through other people, develop an action plan. An action plan on the job is a statement of the logical, step-by-step flow of actions you need to take to effect results.

Factors to consider when creating an action plan:

- What needs to be done?

- Who should do it?

- When is the deadline?

- How will it be done?

Most people pride themselves on being problem-solvers. Successful people reside in the future. They plan, plan and plan some more to determine how goals can be met. An action plan is the fourth step.

Identity → Values→ Goals → Action Plan ——▶ Outcome

Now you are ready to implement your action plan. The fuel that will propel you forward on this journey is motivation.

Motivation

Without motivation even the most well-defined action plans are meaningless. Positive motivation excites, energizes and generates excellence. Motivation is the ingredient that creates success.

In Your Personal Life

Motivation is desire. It is the desire to get out of bed each morning, to take the next step in your action plan, to overcome adversity and be successful. It is the desire to do what is necessary to realize your goals. Motivation is also what drives you to be excellent day after day. We all have different reasons for being motivated (or not motivated); but for each of us, motivation is the key step between defining goals and achieving an outcome.

In Your Professional Life

Often the key question is: How do you motivate people? People behave in a certain way when it makes a difference for them to do so. If you can show another person how he is going to benefit from doing something, you have a motivated employee or co-worker. Learning to motivate effectively is essential to your success. No one works in a vacuum. We are dependent on others directly or indirectly. Step five is motivation.

Identity → Values → Goals → Action Plan

⤷ Motivation → Outcome

Wouldn't it be nice if you could list all kinds of reasons for yourself and others to be motivated and then automatically reach the desired outcome? Unfortunately, it's not that simple. Even the most motivated people suffer from doubt, discouragement and procrastination. The missing ingredient is discipline.

Discipline

Successful people don't succumb to procrastination or temporary setbacks. They call upon an inner strength to overcome obstacles, something everyone has used at one time or another — discipline.

In Your Personal Life

Discipline in your personal life may be the hardest step to take. Whether it involves dieting, exercising or controlling your temper, it's not fun. But it can be learned and developed, and the more you use it, the more you will have control over your life.

In Your Professional Life

The discipline you must adhere to on the job is often not self-imposed. Discipline is hard without organizational controls. With them, it becomes easier. Discipline on the job functions best when it starts at the top – when standards are clear, fair, understood and actually used. If you're lucky, you work where discipline instills pride instead of resentment. Discipline, a tremendous motivator, is step six.

Identity → Values → Goals → Action Plan
↓
Motivation → Discipline → Outcome

Flexibility

Unless the path from identity to outcome is straight and predictable, and it rarely is, flexibility is essential. You must be able to modify your strategies and adapt your action plan when changes occur.

In Your Personal Life

Your personal values evolve as you mature, as your priorities shift and as your family situation changes. By constantly re-evaluating yourself, your values, goals and action plan, you can adapt to change. It would be tragic to work hard and reach a goal only to realize you no longer treasure it.

In Your Professional Life

There are dozens of variables that can change on the job, each of them affecting you in a potentially profound way: a change in pay structure or work hours, a new supervisor or new ownership of the company, to name a few. Each variable has the potential to either set you back or create an opportunity! Successful people know that one key to success is flexibility — step seven on our journey.

Identity → Values → Goals
↓
Action Plan → Motivation → Discipline
↓
Flexibility → Outcome

The destination on your road map is the outcome. You are now more focused, successful and happy if you have mastered each step along the way.

The chapters in this handbook follow the eight-step road map, starting with understanding your true *identity*, to arriving at an *outcome*. You must adapt what you read here to fit your own situation. If you travel through all eight steps, you will almost surely be provided with more achievement and satisfaction than you had before. Each step is essential yet different in terms of its complexity.

Motivation is by far the step that has generated the most debate, study and theories. This book takes a practical approach by boiling motivation down to this: If you are rewarded for doing something, you will be motivated.

In order to learn more about the meaning of motivation, we'll look at various aspects of this extraordinarily complex area.

- A definition.

- Acceptance of people.

- Forms of reward.

- Praise and criticism.

- Involvement.

- Keeping score.

• Self-motivation.

The eight-step system outlined in this handbook heightens your chance for success. Neglecting any of the steps decreases your chance for success. The outcome you define will happen because you make it happen. Begin your journey to higher achievement at step one by telling yourself that there are no shortcuts.

2

IDENTITY: BECOMING AWARE OF WHO YOU ARE

If you have no concept of who or what you are, your journey into the future will be uncertain. Without a well-defined identity, your ability to succeed will depend on luck. Defining your identity will keep you focused as you set priorities, organize tasks, deal with emergencies and accomplish challenges in your personal and business lives.

If you have no concept of your identity, you run the risk of trying to be everything and do everything in a random, haphazard way.

Defining Your Identity

The first step in defining your identity involves self-awareness — seeing yourself as others see you. It involves being honest with yourself, for example, about the quality of your work and your attitude. Taking inventory of yourself can be an uncomfortable and even painful experience, but it is necessary if you want to improve.

The self-inventory should include an evaluation of:

- Your attitudes.

- Your self-image.

- How you treat other people.

As you reflect on these aspects of your life, avoid:

1. ***Defining yourself in terms of external "things."*** It's easy to define yourself by external trappings: cars, clothes, job titles, etc. But what happens to your identity if you lose the expensive car and the powerful job title?

   Focus on the things in your life that endure: the personal relationships that are important to you, the quality of your life, your professional ethics and goals, your personal integrity. Define yourself in terms of elements that are fundamental to who you are and how you behave.

2. ***Defining yourself in terms of "shoulds."*** When we make decisions or behave because we feel we "should," we might be letting others' expectations determine our identity. (Obviously, some "shoulds" are the result of commitments we have made or adherence to laws and social conventions and *should* be honored.) Separate others' expectations from what *you* expect of yourself. Ultimately, you have to be able to comfortably live with yourself.

3. ***Defining yourself in terms of stereotypical "roles."*** It's sometimes easy to let roles determine how we act and see ourselves. But traditional, stereotypical roles such as "wife/mother/nurturer," "husband/father/provider," "career woman" and "corporate executive" can limit our potential. Your various responsibilities are an important part of your self-image, but don't define yourself solely by them.

Defining Your Professional Identity

If you are like many people, you take your job so seriously that your identity becomes closely associated with what you do and where you work. Here are some questions to ask yourself that will help you define and better understand your professional self.

- How do I spend my time on the job? (Different from a job description.)

- What are my people strengths?

- What are my major problem areas?

- Are my skills being fully utilized?

- Do I like the way I'm treated on the job?

By answering these questions, you are better equipped to set and pursue professional goals.

If you are a supervisor and trying to determine your department's identity, you might want to discuss how your group contributes to the larger corporate identity and purpose. A group meeting is an excellent forum to discuss these questions. You want the advantage of hearing from as many people in your group as possible. Involving staff is a great motivator, which we'll discuss later.

Positive change results when a group knows its professional identity. For instance, you can drop activities that cause you to stray from your original mission. Your priorities are clearer and you can work more productively toward a satisfying goal.

When your department or work group defines its identity, each person has a greater sense of purpose and sees his job description more clearly.

Case Study:

Margo is a 27-year-old computer programmer. She amends and

enhances marketing and accounting systems for a large company that manufactures telecommunications equipment. She is divorced and lives in an apartment with a female roommate. As part of a self-examination process, Margo is using the eight-step approach to help define her long-term personal and career goals.

She asks herself a number of questions in order to learn her identity.

1. *How do I feel about myself?* She generally has a healthy degree of self-esteem. She projects a bright, optimistic attitude about life and is cheerful most of the time.

2. *How do people treat me, both on and off the job?* In her personal life, Margo has many friends. She meets people very easily, and they respond to her quickly. She finds it amazing how often people talk to her about very personal matters.

She gets respect off the job, but it's a different story where she works. She gets very little regular feedback from either her boss or her co-workers. Her last performance review was not good. Her boss said she has a bad attitude.

This is in contrast to her natural outlook on life. By considering this question, it allowed her to see clearly, for the first time, the difference in the way she's treated when she's working as opposed to when she's not.

3. *How do I spend my time on the job?* She works at a computer terminal all day long. She has very little contact with other people. At first she found her job stimulating; now she's bored. This explains her poor performance review. She considers her compensation to be fair.

4. *What do I do when I'm not working?* In her spare time, she likes to care for her two parrots and cat, and she often participates in animal rights demonstrations. This is very much unlike her colleagues, many of whom spend their leisure time tinkering with their own personal computers. This often makes her feel like an outcast.

5. *What are my strengths?* Margo knows she is a "people person." She can get along with just about anybody. She's a very caring person, which explains her desire to work with animals. She's also conscientious. Although she is no longer excited about her job, she still takes pride in her performance.

6. *What are my weaknesses?* She has difficulty managing her finances. She usually is a month behind in paying her bills. She's not careful about her physical appearance. She's a few pounds overweight and has never been disciplined enough to do anything about it. She is not ambitious, and blames that for not having a game plan to change her situation.

Margo is doing what every person and organization must do periodically. She is examining herself honestly. She is becoming aware of her own identity, which is step one on the road map.

You will follow Margo as she progresses along the eight-step path toward a better life and higher achievement.

Identity ————————————————▶ Outcome

When you become aware of your identity, you might not like what you see. One reason is that your identity is not consistent with your values, which is the subject of the next chapter.

3

HOW TO DETERMINE YOUR VALUES

How would you like to dream for months about going on a great vacation and then have a miserable experience? The same thing can happen if the objectives in your life are not based on sound values. The outcome you achieve may leave you feeling dissatisfied and empty.

What are values? They are your most important fundamental beliefs. For a society, values are the basis for many laws that dictate our behavior. Such things as murder, theft and assault are actions that violate society's common values. Society's values, and by extension its laws, provide us with structure that helps us organize our lives.

If you clarify your values, you create a basic structure upon which you can build your personal life, your career and all other important aspects of your life. Values go by different names:

- Principles
- Purpose
- Convictions

- Ideals
- Beliefs

Whatever you call them, you must understand your values before you can formulate meaningful goals and your action plan.

Your Personal Values

Defining your personal values is a difficult process. It is only through value clarification, however, that you make your life meaningful. Here are some questions that will help you determine your personal values.

- What is my attitude toward other people?

- What three moral issues are important to me?

- What are my obligations to community, country and family?

- What values do I want to instill in my children?

Your answers will help you identify your fundamental values and how they affect your personal relationships. Successful people know there is much more to life than just getting by or earning a living. You must look inside yourself and determine what is important to you. You should do it frequently. Defining your values gives you the energy and focus to pursue your goals.

Professional Values

If your organization doesn't operate on sound values, each employee has an excuse to cut corners or perform less than honestly or ethically. If an organization instills sound values and insists that those values be a part of daily life from top management on down, it can be a tremendous motivating force and bring people together as part of a team working for a common purpose.

Case Study:

Margo has committed the time and energy to work on her values.

In defining her values, she concentrated on four key areas.

- Her relationships with others.

- Her work environment.

- Her contribution to society.

- Her priorities in terms of personal fulfillment.

To determine her values in each of these four areas, she asked herself the following questions.

1. *How important is having contact with people, especially on the job?* She determined that relationships with friends and co-workers are more important to her than they are for most people. She finds this ironic, because as a computer programmer she has very little interaction with people. Many of her colleagues distrust others and the unpredictable way people often behave. They seem to find comfort in the logic of their computers. Margo isn't bothered by the illogical quality of human nature, and is very trusting and accepting of people.

2. *What do I value most in a work environment?* Margo has a good friend who genuinely loves her job. During one conversation, she was given an example of why her friend thinks her job is so great. She said that on her birthday she received a card with a warm, handwritten message from her boss. Her friend said this is typical of the way she is made to feel special at work. Margo determined that her friend's work environment is very much like Margo's own personality — warm and friendly — and that she would fit very nicely into a similar work environment.

3. *Do I feel a need to make the world a better place?* Yes. Margo has a strong need to help others, especially those who can't help themselves. For her, this means animals. She has strong empathy

toward them, and values the opportunity to relieve suffering for those creatures that can't help themselves. She feels very little of this need is being satisfied in her current situation.

4. *What are my priorities in terms of personal fulfillment?*
Money is not as important to her as other things. She places great emphasis on experiencing joy and having a positive attitude about life, which she affirms frequently at her church. Her belief in a positive mental attitude is evident almost all the time, except when she is working. Friendships also matter a great deal to her. And since she's not interested in forming romantic attachments for the time being, her appearance and health are secondary. She is not ambitious in the standard sense. Quality of life and work are important to her.

As a result, Margo concludes that her values are:

• Cultivating and maintaining strong personal relationships with friends, family members and co-workers.

• A preference for a warm, emotionally supportive work environment. She might be willing to take a lower salary to achieve this.

• Committing her time and energy to help animals that are sick, hurt, abandoned, abused or need nurturing.

• To be surrounded by positive people and influences, reflecting her own positive attitude.

Determining values is the second step on your road map to success.

Identity → Values ———————————————→ Outcome

Establishing values allows you to set goals in order of priority. Without values, all goals are equally important. Goal-setting is the subject of the next chapter.

4

DEFINING YOUR GOALS

If you've ever tried to plow a field, you know this to be true: If you don't look at a fixed point on the horizon, your rows will meander all over the field.

The same is true in your life. Without keeping sight of a specific goal, you are likely to wander off course. This is probably not the first time you've been told you need goals if you want to be successful. Most people have heard this advice. And yet less than five percent of the population sets goals. Why?

1. *It's hard work.* It requires time and soul-searching, which most people are unwilling to do.

2. *Fear of failure.* If you don't set goals, you can't fail. True. But you can't succeed either. You can overcome fear of failure by giving yourself permission to fail. Failures teach you how to be successful.

3. *Fear of success.* This is a very complex fear. Some people don't value themselves enough to feel they deserve success. Others don't set goals because they are unwilling to make the sacrifices necessary to achieve their goals.

We all have fears. If you find yourself saying, "I don't have enough time" or "I don't have the education" or "Too many others are after the same thing" or "I'll just be criticized for being a dreamer," understand that these are all excuses. You have the potential to be whatever you want to be, but you first have to decide what that is. It's not enough to merely set goals. You have to do it correctly. What follows are guidelines for setting effective goals.

In Your Personal Life

1. *Goals should be an extension of your values.* When goals support what you believe in, life becomes truly exciting. Goals based on values make it easier for you to determine your priorities. You can have as many as 50 or 100 goals. But prioritize them using the "front burner/back burner" system.

   - Front-burner goals have the highest priority. You should focus on no more than two or three front-burner goals at a time.

   - Back-burner goals have a lower priority. As you achieve your front-burner goals, move the back-burner goals up the priority ladder.

2. *Goals should be specific.* Goals such as happiness, success, wanting to travel more and wealth are too vague to be effective. Here are some examples of specific goals.

   - To have a net worth of $200,000 by the time I'm 40 years old.

   - To graduate from college by next May.

   - To lose 25 pounds by the end of the year.

- To spend three weeks in Australia next summer.

Your goals are specific when they are also measurable. Each of the above goals has a defined objective and deadline that allows you to measure your progress.

3. *Goals should be written.* Having goals that exist only in your mind is merely wishful thinking. Writing down your goals represents a commitment.

4. *Set challenging but realistic goals.* Big goals always precede big accomplishments. But be realistic. Don't shoot for earning 10 million dollars next year if you are currently making $15,000. Don't pledge to be president of your company by the end of the year if you are now a file clerk.

When you dream big, it's also a good idea to be careful with whom you share your goals. Many people laugh at dreamers, so keep your goals to yourself or share them only with supportive people who can help you achieve your goals.

5. *Visualize your goals.* Form a vivid mental picture of your goals. This may sound difficult, but you can train yourself to do it. If your goal is to own a new house by this time next year, visualize your new home down to the smallest detail: color, size, landscape and yourself in it.

This is an extremely powerful technique. The more details your visualized goals contain, the easier it is for the subconscious to embrace them. When something is hammered into your mind in clear detail, it becomes part of your reality. When your mind accepts your visualized goal as reality, you will work long and hard to achieve it.

6. *Reward yourself.* This provides incentive and helps overcome roadblocks such as procrastination. Figure out ahead of time how you'll reward yourself after you accomplish your goal. Some examples:

- Promise yourself dinner at your favorite restaurant.

- Plan a vacation after you earn your MBA.

- Throw a big party after remodeling your house.

In Your Professional Life

The same goal-setting guidelines that work in your personal life also apply to your career.

1. ***Base your career goals on values.*** More than ever we are looking for meaning, fulfillment and personal growth in our lives. And we're demanding those qualities in our jobs as well. An organization that understands this tends to have a happier and more productive workforce. If an organization has a clearly articulated statement of philosophy and values, there can be a meshing of corporate and personal goals known as alignment.

   Your professional goals will take on a sense of mission when they are consistent with not only your deeply held beliefs, but with the values of your organization as well. If you are a supervisor, allow your staff members to shape group values. As a result, your goals, the goals of other people and the organization's goals take on a new dimension. They are motivating because they are integrated.

2. ***Set specific departmental goals.*** Examples of goals that are too vague:

- Increase productivity.

- Decrease turnover.

The same goals could be stated:

- Increase the department's average daily quota 15 percent by the end of the fiscal year.

- Decrease turnover by March to less than 10 percent annually from the current rate of 28 percent.

Each of these goals is measurable and has a deadline, which is characteristic of specific goals.

3. ***Write down professional goals.*** Keep them simple and easily understood. Write out goals in one memorable, concise statement. When goals are concise, they are easier to understand and communicate to others.

4. ***Set attainable goals.*** Dream big but be realistic. Goals that are out of reach only cause frustration.

5. ***Lead others by example.*** Be as positive about accomplishing a goal as you can be. Describe the desirable outcome for others as vividly as possible. If you supervise employees, share your vision with them, and the goals will become a powerful motivational tool.

6. ***Establish rewards.*** Let people know in advance that they will receive some kind of reward when a goal is realized. Be creative. It doesn't have to be money. It can be:

- A party.

- An award.

- An ad in the local paper.

- A day of training to further their careers.

- A day off.

- A special privilege like a reserved parking space.

Case Study:

It's now time for Margo to engage in goal-setting. She doesn't like her job. It's too impersonal. She likes people and animals, and she has contact with neither in her current job. She has investigated occupations where she could work with animals, but in most cases, the salaries are too low. The one exception, becoming a veterinarian, involves too many years of study.

Recently she discovered that most animal doctors employ veterinary technicians. Margo would have to go to school for six months to get certified as a vet tech, but she could keep her current job in the meantime.

Her peer group would then be other people who share her love of animals. Furthermore, her people skills would be utilized by the contact she would have with pet owners. She visualizes herself in a white coat, helping save an animal's life, then seeing the smile and gratitude of a happy pet owner. She likes what she sees in her mind's eye.

A veterinary technician earns less than she currently does. However, within two years, she plans on becoming the head technician, which would put her just about at her current salary level. In addition, she would receive free veterinary care for her pets. She believes she'll be making enough money to finally manage her financial problems.

Margo's goals are:

- To be a veterinary technician in six months.

- To pay all bills within 90 days.

- To save $1000 in the next year.

- To make at least one good new friend each month.

Step three on the road to success has been completed.

Identity ➔ Values ➔ Goal ─────────────➤Outcome

Thinking about goals is necessary for success. But thinking is not doing. How to put your goals into action is discussed in the next chapter.

5

WRITING YOUR ACTION PLAN

You've clarified your identity, discovered your values and set your goals. Now you have to determine the steps necessary to reach your outcome. Goal-setting involves ideas about the future. But an idea has value only when it is acted upon. Planning brings the future into the present so you can do something about it.

An action plan answers this question: What needs to be done to turn goals into reality? Answering this question can be overwhelming. Where do you start? What strategies will work best? What resources will give you the outcome you want?

There are definite steps you can take to make goals reality.

In Your Personal Life

1. *Create a goal activity page.* Write down those actions that will help you complete your goals. Start with the goal that is most important to you. You should have one sheet of paper for each of

your goals. At the top of the first page, write your highest-priority goal. State it concisely and in specific language. On the left side of the page, list all the activities that will enable you to reach that goal. List them in order of importance. In a column to the right of each activity, list who or what can help you accomplish that step. In a third column, write a target date for accomplishing each activity. (There is a sample form included in this chapter that you can use as your activity page.) On another activity page, do the same thing with the goal that is your next highest priority. Develop these activity pages for as many of your front-burner goals as you feel you can reasonably accomplish. Do not do too many or you will get intimidated by the large number of activities.

2. *Start now.* NOW is the secret word of success. Don't wait. As soon as you have developed goals, prioritize them and write your action plan. Begin taking the necessary steps that will move you toward the completion of a goal. The best place to start is with the first activity that corresponds with your most important goal. Focus on it, then do the following:

- Spend a minimum of five minutes each day doing the first activity listed under your top goal.

- Don't wait until conditions are perfect. They never will be. Expect problems. Tackle each one as soon as you encounter it.

- If you fear taking action, don't look at all the steps ahead of you. Concentrate on only one at a time. Focus just on what is required to complete a single activity.

In Your Professional Life

Planning is an essential ingredient of a good supervisor. Leadership means being in control, and nothing will put you in control better than having an action plan for accomplishing your professional and departmental goals.

Yet most of us don't spend enough time planning. Often it's because:

- It's easy to get caught up in day-to-day operations. Putting out today's fires is often more critical than thinking about tomorrow. Ironically, putting out fires means we are not focusing on what's important: fire prevention – taking steps to avoid future problems.

- It's easy to believe that planning should be done at the highest levels of an organization. Not true. Planning is an everyday activity; it's something that should be done with your organizational group no matter the level or size.

- Planning takes a commitment of time and energy. But if you don't plan, you'll find yourself wasting time and energy doing the things that could have been avoided.

For your job or departmental action plan:

1. ***Write it down.*** You may need to use a planning sheet that's more detailed than the one in this book, but the format should be the same. For each goal, list all activities necessary to accomplish it, then list who or what it will take to get them done. Then decide on a timeframe. It's a good idea to keep action plans in a loose-leaf notebook and make them an integral part of your entire time management system.

2. ***Begin now.*** Develop your action plans immediately, and review and use them on a daily basis. This builds confidence in leadership, and consequently, the people you work with will be more motivated. Action plans tell you what to do today in order to solve — or avoid — tomorrow's problems. They are fire prevention. They not only tell you what to do, they also tell you what not to do. By saying "yes" to a project or course of action, you are also saying "no" to something else less important. Action plans tell us what needs to be done right now that is the best use of our time.

Case Study:

Margo's most important goal is to change careers. Her goal at the top of her activity page reads: To become a veterinary technician within one year.

Here is a list of her activities:

- Get literature on schools that offer courses in becoming a vet tech. Deadline — two weeks.

- Apply for admission. Deadline — one month.

- Apply for financial assistance. Deadline — one month.

- Start school at night. Deadline — two months.

- Graduate. Deadline — eight months.

- Search for job and get a job. Deadline — 10 months.

- Earn first paycheck as a vet tech. Deadline — 12 months.

Margo completes other activity sheets that allow her to better manage her finances, form new relationships, improve her physical appearance and deepen her spiritual commitment. A sample of an activity sheet for Margo's initial stages of her new career is provided. She has taken the fourth step on her road map to success:

Identity → Values → Goals → Action Plan ⟶ Outcome

Your action plan is part of the motor that will drive you on your journey to success. The motor now needs fuel. The "fuel" is motivation and it's the next step on your road map.

Action Plan

Goal: _____

Activities (must be done to achieve goal)	Resources Needed (money, people)	Target Date

6

THE MEANING OF MOTIVATION

Is it really possible to motivate others? This question has generated debate for years. Some experts say that by providing encouragement and incentives, you can motivate someone else. Other experts say you can't motivate others — motivation comes from within.

The debate is meaningless. This book takes a much more practical approach. Its assumption is: *People don't behave in a particular way without an incentive.*

Let's say you have a choice between two activities. Option A has certain benefits, and Option B has certain benefits. Which would you choose? You look at the reasons for doing one as opposed to the other. Whichever option gives you the most reward is the one you would select.

Supplying Rewards for Another Person

Rewards are sometimes known as consequences. If the consequence of a behavior is something a person wants or needs badly enough, then motivation exists. If you want to change someone's behavior, change the consequences.

Managers often try to change attitudes. They use quick-fix programs or "rah-rah" speeches. These invariably fail. But changing the reward or consequence will change behavior. You'll see a more productive employee. And by focusing on rewards and behavior, you can improve attitude.

Researcher B.F. Skinner learned about this concept in an experiment with rats. If a rat pressed a lever, it was rewarded with food. The food was the consequence of the behavior. And before long, the rat was a busy little lever-pusher. Skinner was known as a behaviorist, and what he discovered was a sure-fire way to motivate humans as well.

Human beings are obviously different from rats, and so a food pellet isn't going to do the trick. What will?

The best rewards are those that meet people's basic needs and wants. So the key question is: What do people want and need? Some general wants and needs are:

1. Love and acceptance.

2. Satisfaction from work.

3. Approval of others.

4. Involvement with a group.

5. Feedback on job performance.

These five basic needs correspond to the next four chapters in this handbook. Each will be examined in depth. In addition, there is a chapter on self-motivation. If you want to reduce motivation to its essence, it's this:

To the degree you give others what they want,
they will give you what you want.

The key to successfully motivating others is first to give on your part. A manager who says, "I'd give Mike more praise if he would just do a better job," has it backwards. He must give praise and recognition first (to *something* Mike does well) in order to bring forth the extra effort from him.

This approach takes patience, practice and faith. There are several steps:

- Determine what the person needs.

- Present it at the appropriate time.

- Supply the reward in the appropriate way.

- Be willing to give up something to get something.

These are all motivational factors that will be discussed later.

It's been pointed out that no one does anything without a reason. Thus, when someone starts a new job, that person is motivated. Getting the job has satisfied whatever needs the person had for seeking the job: money, opportunity, challenge or career advancement.

Managers usually don't realize that new employees are a great motivational opportunity for them. This opportunity may be short-lived because the person also brings to work personal as well as work-related needs and interests. When people feel that a person or an organization doesn't consider their needs or interests, it is difficult to motivate them.

In Skinner's rat experiment, the consequence (food) was used to motivate the animal toward a particular behavior. You can also change the consequence so that someone is demotivated from an undesirable behavior and motivated toward something more desirable. This demotivation is known as a threat or punishment. In other words, if you don't like what someone is doing, make the consequence of the behavior unpleasant to that person, and the person will stop doing it.

But negative motivation can backfire. People can become stubborn and resentful when they sense they are being treated in a negative way. They might seek revenge instead of making a positive change. In some circumstances, the negative attention may be perceived as being better than no attention at all and actually cause an increase in the behavior you are trying to eliminate.

When changing behavior by changing the consequence, emphasize positive reward rather than punishment. Obviously punishment is appropriate in some situations, but the reaction to punishment, threats or harsh criticism tends to be excuses, refusal of responsibility and in some cases, outright aggression. All of this tends to decrease the level of performance you want.

Case Study:

You can now apply what you know about motivation to Margo. The behaviorist explanation for motivation fits her case perfectly.

Her needs were not being met as a computer programmer. It was too impersonal an environment for her. She looked into the future and saw that the rewards were greater for her as a vet tech. So she decided to change. She expects to be more motivated at her new job because she'll have more contact with people and be able to work with animals. Her emotional needs will be met at her new job. With the change of consequence, her behavior and attitude will change.

Before you can change your behavior or someone else's, you need to identify and realize a benefit or payoff.

Motivation is step five on your journey to success.

Identity → Values → Goals
↓
Action Plan → Motivation ⟶ Outcome

It's an ancient question: Are people motivated for love or for money? You'll learn the answer in the next chapter.

7

MOTIVATION: FULFILLING PERSONAL AND EMOTIONAL NEEDS

Four Primary Motivation Methods

1. *Fear.* Threatening an employee with the loss of a job, a bonus or a raise. You may get results – once. But you'll get resentment forever.

2. *Incentive.* Providing a bonus or trip to Hawaii, etc. But after the reward has been given, what is the incentive to continue producing?

3. *Attitude.* You must present a reason for a change in attitude.

4. *Fulfilling Personal Needs.*

One approach that has consistently proven to be the most effective is fulfilling personal needs.

To get the best results, you must try to match the individual to the type of motivation that best suits him. Ideally, this match also fits the requirements of the job so that the outcome is a true "win-win" situation: the employee has his emotional needs met, and the organization has its productivity needs met.

Eight Basic Personal Needs

The list of personal needs is as long as there are people, but here are eight basic needs that many of us feel.

1. Belonging. Being part of a group provides us with a sense of comfort, security and partnership. When we belong, we share experiences with others, which provides emotional enrichment.

2. Achievement. Everyone needs to feel a sense of accomplishment. It gives our lives purpose, and it reinforces our self-esteem because it demonstrates our competence.

3. Advancement. Advancement is a measure of our success. To feel successful, we need to feel as if our lives are expanding and our careers are moving forward.

4. Power. This is tied to advancement because an advance in a career usually means more power or increased authority.

5. Responsibility. With responsibility comes respect, both for the person given responsibility and for the person who delegated it. And self-respect is a very powerful motivator.

6. Challenge. We need challenge to grow mentally and emotionally, personally and professionally. The alternative is to stagnate, which breeds negativism, low self-esteem and dissatisfaction.

7. Recognition. Knowing we did a good job is important, but having others know it as well is essential. Otherwise, we feel as if we are living and working in a vacuum. A letter or memo, an award, a gift or a bonus are all forms of recognition. Reserve this for the above-average performance.

8. *Excellence.* Along with the need for self-esteem comes the need to be proud of our work and accomplishments. Doing an excellent job is often a reward in itself, which explains why millions of workers can find joy in their work even when it's routine.

By being attentive to these eight personal needs you can provide job enrichment for an employee. When a person's emotional needs are met, it is called self-fulfillment, and it means that person is approaching his potential. But it's essential to match the employee to the type of motivation.

Taking Care of Emotional Needs

Money is important to people. The paycheck enables an individual to purchase the necessities vital to survival, as well as the comforts of life. In addition to a paycheck, employees are also paid in the form of fringe benefits such as insurance and retirement plans.

Some supervisors believe that employees should be motivated if a company pays them good wages and offers ample fringe benefits. It rarely works that way.

If higher pay and generous fringe benefits were enough to boost performance levels, then General Motors would be out-performing Toyota two to one. It isn't so because the rewards that motivate people aren't solely monetary. There are other less tangible motivators. They include:

- A memo of appreciation.

- A birthday card.

- Being an accepted part of a group.

- Prompt attention to safety needs.

- Listening to suggestions.

- Sensitivity to personal problems or crises.

Pay hikes and bonuses don't hurt, since we all like what money will buy. But the real reward people want is the sense of emotional fulfillment that makes a job worth doing. If you meet a person's emotional needs, that's a far more powerful motivator than financial rewards will ever be.

Two of the most fundamental needs almost every employee has are:

1. Respect for his ideas, concerns and feelings.

2. Contribution to his sense of self-worth.

A key element in effective motivation is the ability to communicate well. Communication skills are particularly crucial when you are trying to meet the emotional needs of others. You can have the greatest system of controls, practice the latest management theory or spend a year developing corporate strategy, but if you can't communicate with the people you work with and supervise, your efforts will be wasted.

Communicating Respect

All of us want to be respected. One of the best ways you can communicate respect is by developing good listening skills. Effective listening takes practice. It's estimated that we listen at about a 25 percent efficiency level. We let external noises distract us and don't make an effort to understand the true message someone is trying to communicate.

Effective listening takes commitment and energy. If you don't commit to being a good listener, you can't be a good motivator. To turn people on, you have to understand their unique needs, which is impossible if you're not listening.

The 10 Commandments of Effective Listening

1. *A good listener says:* I want to listen. I know listening is not easy. I will not let my mind wander. I will focus all my attention on the speaker. I will make this person feel important when I listen, and as a result I know the person is now eager to cooperate with me.

2. *A good listener says:* My goal is to respect the speaker. I will refrain from making judgments. I value the whole message, the good and bad. Only then will I understand the true person and what he is trying to communicate. I will make a genuine attempt to see the world as he sees it.

3. *A good listener says:* I will use all my physical tools to show that I'm a good listener. My body and my eyes will demonstrate to the speaker that he has my full attention. I will use gestures, such as smiling and nodding, that encourage the speaker.

4. *A good listener says:* I know that words are deceptive, so I will watch for clues in body language. I will listen for tone, volume and inflection. I will try to imagine what the other person is experiencing. I will shut out all external distractions and my own thoughts, prejudices and emotions.

5. *A good listener says:* I will strive for accuracy. To do so, I will confirm what the other person says by practicing "reflective listening." An example is, "It sounds as if you're excited about your promotion." If I'm correct, the person is encouraged to talk. If I'm wrong, it's an opportunity for the speaker to correct me. Either way, accuracy is ensured.

6. *A good listener says:* I will listen with an open mind. This means putting aside biases, prejudices and assumptions. This takes courage because I might be exposed to a new way of thinking. I will resist giving advice. If I am a mirror to the other person's thoughts and emotions, I've provided that person with a great problem-solving tool.

7. *A good listener says:* I am in control. If I feel myself getting angry, I will express only what I know to be true and how it makes me feel. I will not argue with someone. I will look for things to agree with and then build from there.

8. *A good listener says:* I will make people feel important by remembering names and things they tell me.

9. *A good listener says:* I will practice good listening. Listening is a learned skill. The more I practice, the better I will become. I will stress the importance of listening at work and set an example for others.

10. *A good listener says:* I will listen to myself. If I hear negative thoughts, then I will stop them from becoming words and hurting my co-workers. I will program my inner computer with positive thoughts, which greatly improves my chances for success.

Enhancing Another's Self-Worth

The second basic need effective motivators focus on is another's self-worth. You can produce positive behavior in others if the reward or consequence you offer is a heightened sense of self-worth. You can do this by using encouragement.

Encouragers inspire others by their words and actions. When praise or feedback is given to an employee or co-worker, the encourager makes sure it is descriptive. Rather than merely saying, "Good job," the encourager says: "I was impressed at the amount of detailed information included in your report. It was well-written and informative. I know you spent a lot of time working on it. Good job."

Encouragers do five important things to enhance self-worth in others:

1. Have measurable, realistic, meaningful goals.

2. Allow people to participate in a task — to "own" it.

3. Use training as an opportunity to stimulate excitement.

4. Allow their own self-confidence to motivate others.

5. Make sure goals are understood by those working to achieve them.

Case Study:

Margo is now enrolled in night school. She likes it but it's more difficult than she thought it would be. She's having trouble finding the self-discipline to work her full-time job and also study at night. She is becoming discouraged, and talks to one of her instructors.

He listened to her doubts and lack of confidence about completing the program because he was a good listener. And he went a step further. He told her she was one of his best students and convinced her it was true. He expressed his confidence in her ability to achieve her goal. He told her of his experience whereby his diligent studies helped him diagnose a dog's illness just from a routine laboratory test he had performed – exactly the type of test Margo was having difficulty learning. He was rewarded with sincere gratitude from the dog's owner and with a small bonus from his employer.

He assured Margo that if she studied hard, such rewards would be hers when she put her knowledge into practice. Margo was inspired to study harder because her instructor was a good listener and a good motivator. He told her that it was acceptable to feel a bit frustrated, but gave the encouragement she needed to overcome her problem.

Meeting people's emotional and personal needs is step five on the road map to success.

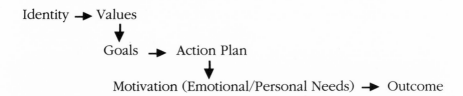

While part of successfully motivating others involves meeting their emotional and personal needs, another equally important aspect involves giving effective praise and constructive criticism. That's the subject of Chapter 8.

8

MOTIVATION THROUGH PRAISE AND CRITICISM

Everyone wants to know how he's doing. You may have done the world's greatest job setting goals and instructing your employees, but you and your group are bound to fail unless you take one major step: provide feedback.

Praise and criticism are two of the single most important functions of a supervisor. Feedback, when misused, can destroy a worker's morale. When handled properly, feedback can motivate even your most lethargic employee.

People change their behavior when the consequences change. Increase the rewards, improve the behavior. Managers motivate others by using praise and constructive criticism, and demotivate others by short-changing their employees or giving rewards unfairly.

Praise

We all want the approval of our fellow human beings. But praise must be given correctly to satisfy and nurture a positive attitude.

An exercise that will prompt you to use praise more often and more effectively than you have in the past is to sit down and write a list of all the good things about each of your employees or co-workers. Your list for each one should contain at least 10 items. Make these items as specific as possible. If you do this, you'll have no shortage of reasons to praise people. This exercise will make it easier to praise in an approximate 10:1 ratio over criticism.

Practice these techniques when giving praise:

- *Be Descriptive.* As mentioned in the previous chapter, the more detail you can build into your positive comments, the greater the impact. Comments like "good job" or "that looks good" can be perceived as token. Take the time to tell an employee exactly why you think he did a good job and why his report looks good.

- *Put It in Writing.* When appropriate, put your praise in writing. This can be anything from a short, handwritten note to a formal letter or memo that becomes part of the employee's file. Putting praise in writing is long-lasting. An employee can reread your note, show it to his family and friends or display it proudly. When you write a memo or letter praising an employee, don't forget to send copies to others who may have been affected by the employee's efforts.

- *Make Your Praise Timely.* Don't wait until an annual performance review to tell an employee he is doing a good job. Praise promptly when you see an employee exhibiting behavior you want to encourage. A performance review should be a time to reinforce the messages you have been giving an employee (praise and constructive criticism) all year.

- *Praise Regularly.* One way to reinforce positive behavior in children is to "catch them being good." A similar approach can be used for employees. Don't wait until an employee does something exceptionally good to praise. Make short, descriptive praise a regular part of your interaction. For example, if you notice an employee has arrived early for work or is staying late to finish a project, verbalize your appreciation. If you see an employee making an extra effort to help a customer or a fellow employee, acknowledge it.

Criticism

Criticism can be a motivator if communicated correctly. It must be constructive criticism, which is difficult for many people. Not knowing how to criticize can result in inappropriate behavior, resentment or even bitterness on the part of the employee. Here are some guidelines.

- *Solve Problems*. Discuss how to avoid the same mistake again instead of berating someone for what has already happened.

- *Avoid Personal Attacks*. Concentrate on behavior, not personalities. Describe in detail the behavior you expect from the employee.

- *Ask for Agreement*. Seek genuine agreement for the changes you've described. Encourage a desire to perform better the next time.

- *Act Promptly*. Deal with problems promptly once, then put them aside. Rehashing old problems will seem more like persecution than constructive criticism.

- *Discuss Problems in Private*. Unlike praise where a public display is often appropriate, criticism should be delivered in private. Whenever possible, avoid embarrassing an employee.

- *Be Positive*. Encourage the person by expressing your confidence that the next time the job will be done properly.

- ***Don't Mix Praise and Criticism***. It only confuses the employee and dilutes the force of both. Praise when deserved, criticize when necessary.

Case Study:

Margo is liking her job in computers less and less with time. One reason is the way her supervisor treats her, always finding fault. The other day he yelled at her in front of other employees for taking so much time to learn the basics of new software.

She feels much better about the way she's treated at night school. When she recently made a mess in the lab, the instructor pulled her aside and very patiently explained how to do her exercises while cleaning up at every step. She looked forward to her next lab session. When she neatly and successfully completed her assignment, her instructor told her exactly why he was proud of her work.

Praise and criticism can both be powerful motivators on the path to success.

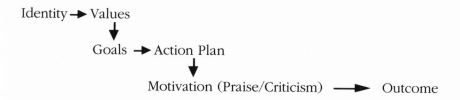

Effective motivators go out of their way to give praise. It makes them feel good, and they know it does the same for others. Motivators also don't avoid handing out criticism, but they do so sparingly and with care. Motivators also know the power of involvement – the subject of Chapter 9.

9

USING INVOLVEMENT TO MOTIVATE

In the past, "top down" management was the rule. Organizational goals were set in the ivory tower, and bureaucratic procedures were mandated to get the job done. Workers were told to follow orders. Their input was rarely solicited, but...

- Who knows most about the problems in the workplace?

- Who has greater knowledge of customers' needs?

- Who knows more about safety needs?

Answer: the worker. The people at the bottom of the chain of command: the clerks, customer service representatives and factory workers. They are a vast resource barely tapped by management. People doing the work know more about the company's problems and needs than anyone else.

Front-line employees' opinions are being solicited more and more because...

- Attitudes toward authority are changing. Workers are demanding to be heard.

- Workers expect to participate in planning. They're better educated and have good ideas they expect will be listened to.

One of the most effective ways to build a sense of employee pride, teamwork and motivation is for supervisors to seek advice, suggestions and information from employees concerning ways in which work should be performed and problems solved.

Contemporary management is now asking all levels of the organization to become involved in these functions:

- Helping determine a company's mission and objectives.

- Analyzing organizational structure.

- Formulating long-range goals.

- Organizing meaningful jobs related to the company's mission.

- Suggesting methods of change.

- Developing short-range plans.

Work groups can contribute to decision-making and planning. This doesn't mean allowing the workforce to make all decisions. It also doesn't mean "faking it" by asking for input and then ignoring it. Participatory management means seeking employees' opinions whenever possible and keeping an open mind to the suggestions and criticisms they offer.

Benefits of Participatory Management

1. *It's a powerful motivator.* When employees feel they are part of a team and have a significant influence on decisions, they are more likely to accept the decisions and seek solutions to difficult problems. In short, they own what they do and where they work. It becomes their company. Pride of ownership translates into a conscientious, hard-working group of people.

2. *Better decisions result.* The more facts you have available when making a decision, the better equipped you are to make a sound one. Participatory management means you have facts coming from all directions. This is sometimes called the Synergy Effect. Or, as it's more commonly expressed, two heads are better than one.

3. *A trusting climate is created.* An environment of trust develops when two people have respect for each other's judgment. The two people in this case are the manager and the employee. It is important for the subordinate to know not only what is being done, but *why.*

4. *Employees understand their jobs better.* If you are a manager, ask your employees to write descriptions of their jobs, including specific responsibilities. Also ask them to prepare at least three job objectives. Use these descriptions to help define responsibilities and objectives so you both understand them.

5. *Progress toward goals is accelerated.* Once objectives are established, the manager and the subordinate should have frequent discussions about how the work is progressing. Their conversations should be as partners in getting the work done. Two-way dialogue is an essential part of involvement. This discussion should address problems, not attack anyone's performance. Good listening should be practiced, and the subordinate's opinion should be respected and accepted.

Participatory management should be practiced all the time, not sporadically. Some organizations have found that formal suggestion programs are helpful. Suggestion programs can provide monetary reward, but a bonus for a good suggestion is only a small part of the overall reward. For many employees, the mere fact that a suggestion has been accepted is a source of tremendous pride.

Employee involvement in many aspects of an organization's operations is the new reality of the 1990s. Even organizations that have been forced to accept this change now find it works to their advantage. They have discovered that group problem-solving and planning almost always produces results far superior to a more centralized form of management.

Case Study:

Margo is now a proud graduate of night school and has earned the right to call herself a veterinary technician. She did such a fine job in serving her internship that the clinic where she worked part time offered her a full-time position.

However, just a few weeks after starting her new job, the owner of the clinic received the financial statements for the previous fiscal year. The clinic was losing money.

All the employees, including Margo, got together to figure out how to stop the flow of red ink. She could not conceive of herself contributing anything of value, since she was a new employee. But as the discussion progressed, she realized that it wasn't the quantity of business that was the problem, but rather the billing system. Different patients were being charged different rates for the same procedure, and often bills weren't sent out for months, much less collected.

Margo drew on her past experience to suggest that a computer be used to standardize rates and produce invoices immediately after a patient visit. If payment doesn't arrive within 30 days, the computer signals that the account needs attention.

Her ideas generated intense excitement at the meeting. Everyone acknowledged that billing was a problem and that computerizing the system was the likely solution. Margo couldn't remember the last time her self-esteem had been so high, and she knew that she was an important new member of a team.

Involvement is a necessary part of step five on your road map to success.

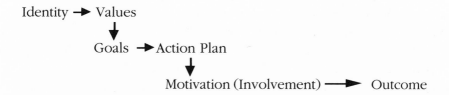

People are motivated when they can see clearly and concisely how they are doing.

10

MOTIVATION: KEEPING SCORE

We live in a sports-crazy world. Many people enjoy following a pro or college team in one sport or another. You may even read the newspaper each day to find out how your favorite team is doing.

But can you imagine following a team or a player if nobody kept score? Would anybody watch the Olympics if medals weren't awarded? Of course not.

Keeping score is a great motivator. When people know how they are doing, they naturally want to do better. Every successful pro team is obsessive about recording performances. It is essential for success.

In business, we keep score differently. Here are some general examples of key performance areas that can be measured:

- Output/productivity.

- Profitability.

- Financial measures commonly found on balance sheets.

- Employee and customer attitudes.

- Market share.

- Sales quotas.

Guidelines to "Keeping Score"

There are several guidelines to follow when you motivate by keeping score:

1. *Share as much information as you can.* Everybody's behavior in your organization contributes to the final score. Therefore, it makes sense to give all employees regular feedback on their job performance and how they're contributing to the final score.

2. *Establish a baseline.* Calculate average performance over a period of several weeks, then post future performance as measured against the average. Also post a goal. People love to see the line on that graph go up with time.

Sample graph:

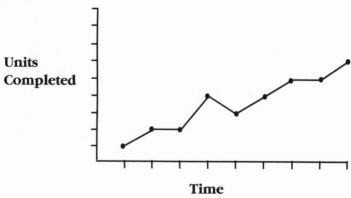

3. *Post performance figures often.* Keeping score is useless unless it immediately follows performance. Too many organizations wait until quarterly or yearly reports come out before reports are posted. Then they have lost much of their motivational value. Post figures as soon as they are available. Establish a specific time when the new figures will be posted (weekly, monthly, etc.).

4. *The information you share should be measurable.* Don't try to chart intangibles such as attitude, enthusiasm or morale. Make it specific. Measure tangibles. Post progress on charts for "units completed." Measure and post only those behaviors or actions you and your employees can see and improve upon: attendance, quotas, quality control.

There are two main benefits of keeping score. First, it shows you are paying attention to people. Second, keeping score is fun. It's fun in sports and it's fun on the job. It brings people together as part of a team.

Case Study:

Margo thought she was doing a good job at the animal hospital, but she wasn't sure. She brought her concern up at a meeting and the ensuing discussion generated a new system of keeping score.

In a veterinary clinic, it's important to use the facilities and the doctor's time as efficiently as possible. This was part of Margo's responsibility. It was decided that, at the end of each week, two graphs would be posted reflecting the output of that week. One measured the number of patients treated each day, another measured average waiting time for the patients. By looking at records kept over a two-week period, they learned that the clinic was treating an average of 30 patients each day with an average waiting time of 20 minutes. The next month's goal was set at 33 patients a day with an average waiting time of 15 minutes. Here is how the graphs looked.

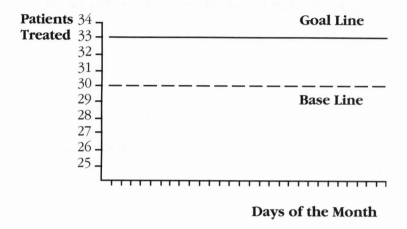

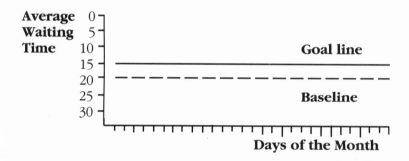

Margo began to experiment with a new way to use exam rooms so that they were in use more often. The graph started to show improvement in the second week. Margo could hardly wait until the end of the week when the data was posted for everyone to see because the trend was up.

Profit and loss statements were also posted, and the bottom line improved. At the end of the month when their goals were reached, the owner of the clinic threw a surprise celebration party. Margo was already part of a team; now she felt as if she were part of a "second family."

Keeping score is an important ingredient in motivating people.

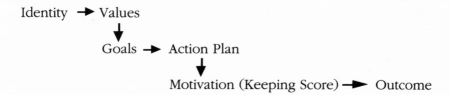

So far, the discussion of motivation has centered on motivating other people. In the next chapter, you'll learn some steps to motivate yourself.

11

SELF-MOTIVATION

To be successful, you must make things happen. You must be self-motivated.

Self-motivation is the bridge between thinking about your goals and accomplishing them. It is the driving force behind high achievement. Self-motivation is desire. It is essential to succeeding in any endeavor.

Motivation is not something that comes naturally for everyone. It can be learned and developed. It is the inner desire that keeps you always moving forward in spite of discouragement, mistakes and setbacks. How do you build this inner desire?

1. **Believe in yourself.** Success and happiness must be part of your self-image. One simple rule will help you do this: Allow only positive thoughts to dominate your thinking, such as:

   • I am worthy.

- I like myself.

- I am strong and self-sufficient.

- I can handle what comes my way.

- I have high but realistic expectations of myself.

- I know the future holds opportunities for me.

- I take total responsibility for myself.

- I am confident that I have the power to confront and resolve problems.

Forcing yourself to think this way may be difficult at first. It takes practice. Stay with it because it becomes easier with time. Only when you believe that you deserve success can it possibly come your way.

2. *Develop the necessary qualities to be motivated.*

- Welcome challenges.

- Have the flexibility to adapt and change.

- Have a sense of pride in your achievement.

- Set goals that are stimulating and challenging.

Motivated people share several qualities. This is the profile of the motivated person. You will find it difficult to be motivated if you don't have these qualities. Develop and use them.

3. *Overcome fear.* Fear is the opposite of desire. Fear creates stress, panic and anxiety, and therefore defeats plans and goals. Here are

some ways you can overcome fear:

- Build self-confidence.

- Identify and understand your fears. Only then can you defeat them.

- Take action. Action cures fear. Once you start to do something, it becomes easier. Your fears will disappear.

4. Start now. Now is the secret word of success. Don't wait until you have more information or the circumstances are perfect. Begin now. Get in motion as soon as possible, and as your momentum builds, so will your motivation.

5. Focus on your rewards. Why should you be motivated? What positive consequences will you enjoy when you put your action plan in motion? Visualize the rewards of success in your mind as clearly and vividly as you can. Make it such a good picture that you'll do almost anything to be part of it. When you drive toward that image you are motivated.

Case Study:

Margo decided to alter her career, lifestyle and financial situation. These changes have caused her doubt and worry. She questions whether she made the right decision.

Since she didn't excel as a computer programmer, she wonders if she'll do well as a veterinary technician. She questions her general competence. Her self-esteem is suffering, and she is finding it difficult to be motivated. Here are the steps she takes to develop self-motivation.

1. *She makes a written contract with herself* to increase her sense of self-worth. Her contract states:

- I have the intelligence to succeed in whatever I try.

- I always strive for excellence.

- I am giving and understanding of others.

- I am building new relationships.

- I am in control of my finances.

- I have the discipline to comply with this contract.

2. *She forms clear mental images* that allow her to see herself in a new way. She visualizes herself as having a warm feeling of inner satisfaction for achieving her goals and overcoming great challenges.

3. *She identifies and confronts her fears.* She has a deep fear of failure. She has taken a big risk in deciding to make changes in her life, and with risk comes the possibility of failure. It can't be avoided, Margo tells herself, and so she has confronted one more obstacle in her journey toward success.

4. *She begins a time-management system.* Each day she fills out a personal time budget. On it are specific times to work on high-priority tasks. It forces her to start now on those things necessary to accomplish her goals.

5. *She thinks about the rewards waiting for her* at the end of her journey. They are many, including working with animals, a better circle of friends and financial responsibility.

The path to success and happiness is rarely an easy one. Make the commitment to work hard for your own personal reasons. Start now, and self-motivation will begin to build within you.

Identity → Values → Goals
                                  ↓

          Action Plan → Motivation (Self) ⟶ Outcome

The most difficult of all the stops on the road map to achievement may be the one discussed in the next chapter: discipline.

12

DISCIPLINE: KEEPING YOURSELF ON THE ROAD TO SUCCESS

Discipline means sticking to an action plan even when there are other things you or your co-workers would rather do. For purposes of this chapter, it means having the necessary self-control to complete whatever tasks are necessary to achieve your goals.

Discipline is hard work. It takes guts. It means staying focused and practicing better work habits. People who get the job done, even when the job is unpleasant, have developed a mental toughness that comes from practice, patience and the ability to see beyond the immediate task.

Discipline must be present for success to occur. Without it there is failure.

Discipline in Your Personal Life

Self-discipline involves doing what *needs* to be done rather than what you would *like* to do. Here are some guidelines.

1. *Take responsibility for yourself.* Only you make it happen. Take responsibility for meeting your goals by taking action.

2. *Don't wait.* Start now. Start small if you have to, but start now. You'll develop momentum, and the task won't seem as hard as you thought.

3. *Practice good habits.* Habits can work for you or against you. Practice self-discipline in small ways: exercise regularly, eat in moderation, schedule time to tackle important unpleasant chores. The more you practice self-discipline, the greater control you have over your life. Developing control over your day-to-day life is the first step in learning that you can also control your success and happiness.

Discipline on the Job

An organization without discipline is doomed to fail. Successful organizations know that discipline means:

1. *Setting an example.* Positive self-discipline must exist throughout an entire management team. Managers cannot expect their employees to practice self-discipline if they don't set an example.

2. *Breaking big jobs into smaller pieces.* If you want to help someone become more disciplined, show him how big tasks can be completed through a series of small steps. Organize projects into manageable segments. If you show a person where to begin and how to proceed, a job becomes less intimidating.

3. *Identifying time-wasters.* Look for time-wasters. Some examples are: not organizing your telephone time (when you return calls, when you make calls), giving in to distractions (visitors, getting coffee, etc.), failing to organize your work before you reach the office, and attending poorly organized, unproductive meetings. Find a good time-management system and use it religiously. Also, look for ways to reduce paperwork.

4. *Focusing on specific goals.* The key to self-discipline is being able to defer your gratification from the present to the future. The best gratification comes when you realize your goals. Reaching a goal is your objective, and practicing self-discipline is the means by which you achieve it.

Case Study:

Margo is now several months into her new job as a vet tech, and the initial excitement is starting to wear off. Her goal is to be appointed the head tech, and she knows she must practice good work habits to earn that promotion. Yet, sometimes she finds herself cutting corners on certain procedures, and she's even shown up late for work a few times.

To make matters worse, her financial situation is still tight. She knows she should be doing better. She's purchased a couple of expensive outfits she didn't need, and at least once a week she stops on her way home from work and buys an album of her favorite music. Just the other day she received a call from a credit card company threatening to cancel her card unless she paid her account.

She decides to change her habits. She hates doing paperwork, but she knows cutting corners could jeopardize her patients' health. She reviews her priorities and reminds herself of her long-range goals. She does this each time she is tempted to cut corners or spend money unnecessarily. Within a few weeks, she doesn't even think about avoiding the paperwork.

She also forces herself to avoid the shopping center on the way home, which helps her in two ways. She doesn't spend as much money, and she's more likely to be in bed early so that she gets to work on time. She begins following the budget she had previously outlined for herself, and at the end of the month she is able to pay all her bills when they are due. Margo is learning discipline.

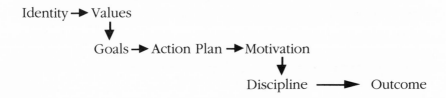

Identity → Values
        ↓
    Goals → Action Plan → Motivation
                           ↓
                   Discipline ⟶ Outcome

The achievement of your goals is now in sight. But in order to be satisfied with your accomplishment, you must be flexible – willing and able to adapt to changing circumstances.

13

FLEXIBILITY: HOW TO RESPOND TO CHANGE

As you move toward your goals, there is one unavoidable facet of your personal and professional life: change.

Sometimes your initial strategy doesn't produce the outcome you want. Or perhaps the goal you first thought was so desirable loses some of its importance. The same thing happens on the job. Your organization or department may find its action plan is flawed, or that an original goal no longer has the priority it once had. Here are three key aspects of change.

1. Change is constant and unavoidable.

2. Change creates fear.

3. People tend to resist change.

Change is frightening because it threatens our sense of security. It is unfamiliar, and we don't like it. It represents a risk. The key to handling change is the ability to adapt. Your survival and that of your organization is directly related to your ability to adapt to change.

Change in Your Personal Life

Changes may be subtle or drastic. Change can become a positive force in your life if you learn coping techniques. Here are some healthy ways to view and adapt to change.

1. ***See change as an opportunity, not as a problem.*** If you are going to view change as positive, look for the opportunities it offers and remain flexible enough to take advantage of them. Change is growth, and despite the anxiety it causes, it can significantly improve your life if you let it.

2. ***Don't just stand there, change.*** Don't let fear paralyze you. When people are confronted by change, the tendency is to ignore or avoid it. No matter how you try to ignore or avoid it, it won't go away. You make the choice: do nothing and let change happen to you, or look for the opportunities and make it work for you.

3. ***Accept change in your life as normal and positive.*** Re-evaluate your goals daily. Don't be afraid to change them. Be flexible. Always fine-tune your action plan so it fits your goals and values. Don't be so rigid and fearful of change that you pursue a goal that, when reached, holds no reward for you.

Change on the Job

There are a huge number of job variables that can change – some of which you have control over, some of which you don't. They include:

- A transfer.

- A new boss.

- New methods.

- New competition.

- New markets.

- New pay rates.

- New technology.

Some call change progress, but it scares many of us. Therefore, it's possible that change, for any reason, will be resisted by you and your co-workers. The key to coping with on-the-job change is flexibility.

1. ***Re-evaluate goals, values and action plans.*** Search for ways to improve. Be sensitive to subtle changes that may indicate more profound future changes. Are competitors slowing down? Is your product about to be regulated by federal or local laws? Will the changing social or economic forces affect your business? These are important issues to be aware of even if you don't own the company.

2. ***Use knowledge to kill fear.*** Don't underestimate others' ability to adapt. Discuss change with everyone affected as soon as possible. Head off fear, rumors and trouble in advance. Communicate change *before* it happens by telling people:

- What the change will be.

- Where it will occur.

- Who will be affected and in what way.

- Why it is being made.

- When it will go into effect.

- How it will be implemented.

3. *Accentuate the positive.* Don't dwell on problems or how terrible the old way was. Instead, discuss the new opportunities that are available. Be enthusiastic about change. The more positive you are, the more others will approach change the same way.

4. *Be patient.* It takes time for old habits to die and new ones to be born.

5. *Provide reassurance.* People often define their identities by their jobs. Therefore, if you change the job you change them. It's a scary proposition. Let them know you still value and respect them. Their self-esteem will remain intact, and change will be accepted more readily.

Case Study:

Margo is near the end of her one-year plan. She's had her share of ups and downs, but basically she's proud of herself for being on schedule with her initial plan. She's been promised the position of head technician on her anniversary, and the clinic is profitable. She also likes the working conditions and her team members.

Then, just when she had fallen into a comfortable routine, her world threatened to crash around her. The owners of the clinic accepted an offer that "was too good to turn down," and were selling out.

The rumor mill started working overtime. She heard that the new owners were going to cut salaries and were going to bring in some of their own people, so layoffs were probable. Margo feared for her job.

A meeting was called. It was announced that the clinic had been sold and a couple of layoffs would occur, but Margo's job was safe. However, a head tech was being brought in. It appeared that Margo had been frozen out of her promotion.

She accepted the changes as a challenge. She immediately contacted other animal hospitals and was hired at another clinic as a head tech at an increase in salary.

She confronted the changes that frightened her, took the initiative and turned a potentially bad situation into an exciting opportunity.

Identity → Values → Goals
        ↓
    Action Plan → Motivation → Discipline
                            ↓
                    Flexibility → Outcome

You're ready to enjoy the satisfaction that comes with realizing the outcome you've been working so hard to achieve. But there are more hurdles to face, which we'll discuss in Chapter 14.

14

THE OUTCOME OF YOUR JOURNEY

The objective of this handbook is to help you achieve important personal and professional goals. If you followed the success road map I've outlined, you've probably achieved your outcome. To one degree or another, you've improved your life.

Outcome is the destination represented by the eight-step road map. Outcome is the result you created because you approached goal-setting in a systematic and disciplined way.

Evaluate your outcome. Successful people are constantly checking, constantly re-evaluating their performance to see how they can do better. That's what makes them successful.

As you look at what you have accomplished, it may occur to you that your outcome is different from the goals you set for yourself in the beginning. Goals are merely conceptual. Outcome is reality.

When you evaluate the results of your journey, keep a few things in mind.

1. *Hold the outcome in high regard.* Even if you fell short of your initial goals, you gained valuable experience along the way. Self-esteem means valuing everything you are and everything you have done. Cherish your past because it is your springboard to the future.

2. *Take pride in your successes.* If you accomplish your objective, take great pride in your achievement. Revel in it, but don't stop. There are other exciting goals for you to achieve. If you didn't quite reach your objective, look at it this way:

   • At least you tried.

   • All successful people fail. And they've usually failed more than once. Do what they do: give yourself permission to fail. You have learned great lessons. You are now better equipped for success.

   • Don't dwell on it. Forgive yourself.

   • Don't place blame. No one else is responsible for your failure. You are. Blaming keeps you stuck in one place.

3. *Focus on what you did right, not what you did wrong.* Learn from your mistakes and accomplishments. Successful people are not that much more talented, better educated or gifted with greater endurance than other people. They work smarter, not harder. Determine what specific skills produced your best results and develop them.

4. *If this handbook doesn't work for you the first time, try again.* A lot of good ideas were discussed. These ideas can eventually become habits for you, but not right away. Habits take practice and perseverance. Don't give up.

5. *Set another goal.* Now that you've arrived at your outcome, it's time to set another goal. You say you're entitled to rest? Yes, so make a period of rest your first goal, then start on the journey again.

Your journey to success doesn't have an end point. Success is a constant process, never a destination in itself. You should always keep trying to improve and strive for excellence. If you "arrive" at success, then you run the risk of complacency.

Life is growth. It's the effort itself that provides the most satisfaction. Your successes are to be savored, but it's the journey that provides the most excitement and fun. See you on the road!

INDEX

Other Titles from National Seminars Publications:
Desktop Handbooks

Qty.	Item#	Title	Price	Total
	10410	The Supervisor's Handbook	$7.95	
	10415	Balancing Career & Family: *Overcoming the Superwoman Syndrome*	$7.95	
	10416	Real Men Don't Vacuum	$7.95	
	10417	Listen Up: *Hear What's Really Being Said*	$7.95	
	10468	Understanding the Bottom Line: *Finance for the Non-Financial Manager*	$7.95	
	10486	Parenting: *Ward & June Don't Live Here Anymore*	$7.95	
	10488	Service, Service, Service	$7.95	
	10495	How to Manage Conflict	$7.95	
	10496	Motivation & Goal-Setting: *The Keys to Achieving Success*	$7.95	
	10498	How to Manage Your Boss	$7.95	

Business User's Manuals

A New Concept in Training! Business User's Manuals are practical, interactive self-study training resources packed with charts, checklists, self-tests and guidelines to make your learning more effective and your job easier.

Qty.	Item#	Title	Price	Total
	10449	Business Letters for Busy People	$12.95	
	10451	Think Like a Manager	$14.95	
	10452	The Memory System	$12.95	

Sales Tax

All purchases subject to applicable sales tax. Questions? Call 1-800-258-7246

Subtotal	
Sales Tax (see note)	
Shipping and Handling ($1 one item; 50¢ each additional)	
Total	

Name _____ Title _____

Organization _____

Address _____

City _____ State_____ Zip Code _____

☐ Please send me a FREE catalog of National Seminars training resources

Method of Payment:

☐ Enclosed is my check or money order payable to National Seminars

☐ Please charge to: ☐ MasterCard   ☐ Visa   ☐ American Express

Signature _____ Exp. Date _____

Card Number _____

Complete and send entire page by mail to: VIP # 705-10496-092

National Seminars Publications, 6901 W. 63rd St., P.O. Box 2949, Shawnee Mission, KS 66201-1349
National Seminars Publications is a division of Rockhurst College Continuing Education Center, Inc.

Wait, There's More!

National Seminars Publications offers a complete line of career-development and self-improvement products designed to help you reach your career and personal goals. And, every one of these products carries an unconditional guarantee of satisfaction. For a complete catalog, call or write to the address below. Just a small sample of the resources available:

AUDIOCASSETTE ALBUMS:

Qty.	Item#	Title	Price	Total
	116	**Powerful Business Writing Skills** – learn the most important skill for your career advancement on this six-cassette album.	59.95	
	126	**Winning Against Stress** – this six-tape series teaches you how to deal with the stress in your life in a positive way.	59.95	
	199	**Becoming a Promotable Woman** – a six-cassette album, workbook and 500-page best-seller for women on the way up.	79.95	
	119	**LifePlanning** – this life-changing six-cassette album shows you how to set goals and plan your future.	59.95	
	121	**How to Handle Difficult People** – a four-cassette album that helps you understand and deal effectively with difficult behavior.	46.95	
	814	**Assertiveness: The Right Choice** – this four-tape series will teach you to stand up for yourself without stepping on others.	46.95	
	811	**The Power of Effective Listening** – learn to communicate more effectively by mastering the skills of active listening with this four-tape series.	46.95	
	124	**Powerful Presentation Skills** – this six-tape series teaches you how to make presentations like a professional every time.	46.95	
	910	**Project Management** – an eight-tape package that gives you a system to complete projects on time, on track and on budget.	79.95	

VIDEOCASSETTE PACKAGES:

Each video training package comes with a copy of the best-selling book it's based on and an audiocassette of the program.

Qty.	Item#	Title	Price	Total
	639	**How to Supervise People** – Techniques for getting results through others including delegation, motivation, goal-setting and more.	95.00	
	640	**How to Get Things Done** – Strategies for getting the most out of each day. Accomplish more, worry less!	95.00	
	641	**The Write Stuff** – Techniques to make your business reports, memos and proposals more powerful, more effective and easier to write.	95.00	

For information or to order, **CALL TOLL-FREE 1-800-258-7246** or write: **National Seminars Publications**, 6901 W. 63rd St., P.O. Box 2949, Shawnee Mission, KS 66201-1349

National Seminars Publications is a division of Rockhurst College Continuing Education Center, Inc.